STUDENTWISE

'The beginning of the rest of your life ...'

Introduction

Excited? Scared? You're leaving home (probably) to spend the best part of three years (hopefully) in another town at a college or university. If that is true for you, then this booklet is for you, courtesy of the Baptist Union (*the what???*) via your own church or a Chaplain.

Yes, it's one more outcrop on the paper mountain for you to read before ever you get to where you're going. No, it doesn't solve all your problems. Nor does it contain free concert tickets, vouchers, or access to the Internet. It does contain some Useful Information. At least it won't take up much room on your desk.

There now follows a list of contents ...

BEING THERE

Hello, Goodbye

The case is unpacked, and stuffed under the contraption you're supposed to use for a bed. The toothpaste tube is nestling among the small pile of discarded body hairs on the sink. The Olds have driven off (at last...). Someone very tasty has just walked past your open door and entered the next room. It's started ...!

A life in the day of ...

Fresher's Fair. Never before have so many things to join been crammed into so small a space. You go in a mere student. You come out a member of the Break Dancing Society, the Juggling Club, two Sports Teams, three Christian groups (more of those later) and the Philosophical and Literary Debating Organisation. You are dazed. You are carrying 100kg of leaflets. You have met more people than you can remember, and several you would like rapidly to forget.

Food in Hall. The unimpressable sitting in front of the uneatable. What is it about catering-quality chips?? You pause at the vending machine on the way out and buy six Mars Bars with the last of the day's money (more of that later).

First Lecture. Arriving early, you are surprised to discover there are no seats left. The lecturer is wearing a jumper with suede shoulder pads. He announces the subject. Half the students leave to find the room they are supposed to be in. You take a seat, get out a pen, lean over your A4 pad, and share a nervous smile with the person next to you. An hour flies by. Only 2260 (approx.) to go. The first day passes ...The first week is almost over.....help!!

Fact 1: *Everybody* feels the same way you do (especially those who say they don't).

Fact 2: No one knows anything! There *are* too many students on your course. There *aren't* enough desks, computer terminals, library books, direction signs. There *are* lecturers who couldn't teach breathing. There are students who *are* more brainy/stupid/attractive/ugly/nervous/confident than you.

Wish YOU were here...

You wake up one morning feeling guilty and miserable. Here you are at college, two hundred miles away from home, where you've always wanted to be, and you feel......homesick!!! You miss Mom's Spaghetti Carbonara. You miss your little sister (aagh!). You miss Ben the Bearded Collie. You miss (wait for it) your Home Church. You miss the guys.

What do to? Go home? Maybe. But why not start with a phone call? It's cheaper. Why not invite a friend to come and visit? That's cheaper too; they might bring you some food. By all means go home, but don't be surprised if home feels different ("Don't forget - be home by 11.30!"), and you can't wait to get back. Make new friends. **Remember,** *everyone feels the way you feel ...*

So many things,

so LITTLE time ...

The Philosophical and Literary Debating Society was not a success. Two meetings in and you realise you can't tell your Derrida from your Penny Dreadful. Neither can the debaters. And there are so many other things to do. How to cope? Don't be afraid to try things - no one minds if you drop out early on (though it can be a tad inconvenient if you give up on playing Shylock in The Merchant of Venice the night before the dress rehearsal). Remember that some of the yawning void between lectures is supposed to be taken up with work. Take the chance to get involved in something that will stretch you (the Mediaeval Torture Society perhaps?), and make you think: college is supposed to be about ideas - political, spiritual, cultural etc. Join in, and remember, *you have nothing to fear from the truth.* Why not help out at the Student Union?

What happens when one of your new friends turns out to be gay - and what's more he's got a friend who keeps banging on about bringing down the Government? Back in the 1930's they used to recruit spies at University! Your college career is going to introduce you to all sorts of people: different colour, different nationality, different sexuality, different beliefs. Most of them will want to be friends for friendship's sake, and show

I'll show you mine if you show me yours.

your ideas the same respect they have every right to expect from you . . . V e r y occasionally, you might meet someone who wishes to involve you in something dodgy. It needs to be stated loudly that often Christians, for fear of the latter, retreat into cosy Christian circles and miss out on the riches of a wider friendship. You have much to learn from others but much to offer too. **Welcome to the big wide world.**

IF I GO UP 2 THE UNIVERSITY, YOU ARE THERE ...

Cast adrift at college on a sea of uncertinty, Robin Goodbody began to sink beneath the waves of meaninglessness, while the ship began to sink beneath the waves of meaninglessness, while the ship of faith sailed on regardless of his plight ...

Jennifer Brightsoul knew what she knew.

She intended to make sure that everyone she met at college came to know it as well.

Cassy Mastermind never let the truth get in the way of a new idea. By the end of the first term there wasn't a religious group on campus she hadn't blessed with her affirming presence.

God, you will be relieved to know, was waiting for you at College when you arrived! And Christian Union, Chaplaincy, Denominational Societies are usually around to make sure you don't forget it. Which of these you get involved in is up to you. What matters is your attitude. Coming from a lively church with lots of Bible you could react like Robin, once you come across the often bewildering variety of Christian groups on campus. Or, like Jennifer, you could

you could just seek out like-minded people, close your ears and set about converting everyone to your point of view. While the Cassies of this world run the risk of reducing Christian faith to just personal preference.

Thankfully, none of our friends are beyond

hope! Let's not pretend: just by leaving home you run a risk, and one of the things you risk is your faith being challenged, questioned, or neglected. Some people find that they slip easily into student Christian affairs, and end up running the CU in no time! Others try something different to their previous world of Christian experience. Still others, under the pressure of work and other interests, drift away from regular Christian

involvement but may come back later on. Others rebel against their Christian upbringing during college years, and avoid religion like the plague.

And the Chaplains see them all! Your University will probably have a Chaplaincy centre. Numerous higher education colleges also have some Chaplaincy staff. There will often be a local Baptist minister designated as a Baptist Chaplain, or if not you'll be able to find some kind of Chaplain around the place. He or she will always respond if you want to talk about a problem, or for just a chat - regardless of whether or not you turn up at their church!

FAITH

While it is true that being a Christian means being involved with others, it's also a matter of personal faith. Like anything else, it will whither and die if you neglect it. So alongside everything else, if you intend to live your Christian faith while at college, you will simply have to make time...

5

One aspect of college life worth mentioning here is the presence of international students. The Christians amongst them will show you dimensions of Christian living you never imagined. Friendship with someone from overseas can be an enriching experience, **both ways.**

In many places in this country, you are likely to find yourself studying alongside those who follow another religious faith - Judaism, Islam, Hinduism, etc. If you haven't met such people before, you'll be surprised to discover how much you hold in common. For every devout Christian, there's a devoted Muslim. For every Christian enthusiastically witnessing to their Lord, there's a Hindu keen to tell you all about her faith. *They won't listen to you if you don't listen to them ...*

One more thing. Colleges are a recruiting ground for cults. They target one or two campuses in an area. Their members turn up in the Union bars, refectories and common areas, looking for lonely or isolated students. They offer friendship, somewhere to get a meal, someone to talk to. All good stuff. But be warned. They're after more than just your turning up when you feel like it. They want to suck you in to a world of total control. It will feel safe at first, but then comes the business: control of your money, who you spend time with, what you read and watch. One day they'll suggest you join. From then on it's all sweetness and light - Not! Trouble is, when they approach you, they'll sound like Christians - "come and enjoy some: fellowship; mission; Bible study; prayer ...".

The best thing to do is to ask questions *at the very beginning:* "what's your group called?"; "who runs it?"; "can I bring some friends?"; "let me have a leaflet to show to my minister".

This leaflet can't give a list of cult names, they're changing all the time, but they often work in the way described. If in any doubt, ask someone in the CU/Chaplaincy, and **let someone know that you've been approached.**

IF I RISE ON THE WINGS OF THE DAWN ON SUNDAY ...

(fat chance!)

College is a new world: trouble is it can come to seem like the whole world, which it isn't! If your chosen institution is in a big town or city, at least there's a chance you'll get to see the odd bus, factory, shop or pub to remind you that there's more to life than lectures and libraries. If you go to a nice, self-contained campus, nestling in unspoilt countryside (or built on the site of an old gasworks), you could spend the whole of term never seeing anybody over the age of twenty-six (except the odd lecturer), or getting stuck in rush-hour traffic.

It is a good idea to get out and about - even if it's only to go shopping. It is also a good idea to go to church ...

Choices:

One of the big, lively churches where lots of students go. For: lots of students; lots of other people; lots of foodie events; lots of worship (singing, praising, praying, studying); probably a student-worker; families offering to take you home for lunch. Transport arranged. Against: lots of students; easy to get missed; you'll feel like a student; it may be a long way.

One of the (big or small) not-quite-so-lively churches where few or no students go. For: no students! feels 'normal'; often friendly and welcoming; won't treat you like a student; opportunities to get involved. Against: worship probably more traditional; have to make your own way there; can't hide in the corner!

Either way, Christian life is more than just campus life. You're more likely to continue with church after college if you spend time in church during college.

A DEGREE OF STUDY ...

It's a dark, cold Thursday evening in November. Your study desk is thick with sheets of scribbled-on A4. There's a pile of text books spread around on the floor. You've spilt coffee on the corner of one of them already. The draft from the window is making your feet cold. You're a hundred words in to a fifteen-hundred word essay, and you still don't understand the question. The deadline is nine o'clock Friday morning.

This will happen to you ...

Study is the one thing that spoils everyone's college years. Unfortunately the best minds of the last hundred years have failed to come up with a way of getting a degree without doing any, though it's always annoying to discover that the best minds seem to get away with doing the least - which is not the same thing as saying that those who do the least have the best minds. Look out for the friendly soul who spends every lecture asleep in the corner, every evening drinking in the Union bar, and completely ignores you all term, until the day before the assignment deadline, when they declare their undying devotion to you and all you stand for, and ask to borrow your notes/calculations/finished masterpiece. You, good Christian soul that you are, will want to help such people. And boy! don't they know it ...

Rule 1. Don't Panic!
Rule 2. Try and keep control of your out-of-lecture time.
Rule 3. Do talk to others on your course.
Rule 4. Ask questions of your tutor before it's too late.
Rule 5. If you get through your course without working all through the night at least once, you will be Lifted Up To The Highest Place, and many nations will come to your door asking *'How may we find enlightenment, Oh favoured One?'*

It's the economy, stupid

(sign on Bill Clinton's desk).

Er, **sorry to bring this up,** but money makes the student world go round, and you won't have very much of it, unless Daddy's very rich. Scenario: Basic grant (approx. £1800 per annum in 1977 and falling), all fees paid (but the Dearing Report will probably change that!). *Term only* expenditure approx. £60 per week to spend. Yippee!! But hang on a minute ...

The Baptist Union **totally** unrealistic table of student expenditure*

	Essential	Desirable	In your dreams
Daily	Travel, Hall food	Snacks	Drink in bar
	£6	£2	£2
Weekly	Toiletries	Magazine	CD
	£2	£2	£14.99
Termly	Course books	New socks,	Pair of shoes, prezzy
	£50	LemSip, CU fee	for Mum, Visit home.
		£15	£100 and upwards ...
Term Total	**£370**	**£135**	**£350 and upwards ...**
Grand Total	£855 and upwards ...		
Term Grant	£600 and falling ...		
Profit (Loss)	(£255 and upwards)		

*correct(ish) in 1997. If you're reading in 2000 add your telephone number.

Congratulations.

You are now officially in debt. This is the natural condition of student life.
Nay, *all* life ...

SOLUTIONS

	Likelihood of success	Advisability
1. Pray	You have to *ask?*	Go for it..!
2. Ask the Vice-Chancellor	ZERO	Puh*lease!!*
3. Ask Mum or Dad	GOOD (but feels bad)	Never let pride stand in the way of a good pizza.
4. Scrounge off mates	ZERO *(Gerrourrahere!)*	Shows who your friends are.
5. Take out Student Loan	100% (Feels bad, but you get used to it)	Unless your name's St Francis
6. *Still* struggle	100%	We will overcome

Some concluding remarks

There's Always Advice On Hand - See your college's own welfare pack

Don't Forget What You Buy Has To Be Paid For SomeDay

As someone once said, Seek first the Kingdom of God and all these things ...

STUDENT Jobs

Many students make endsmeet by working.**Welcome to McDonald city.** You may have to work, or wish to. It can be good, but ask around first, to get some idea of how others manage, and make sure you get the details before taking on a job. Not every cocktail waitress earning £500 per week has to do lap dancing with nothing on, but it pays to find out what you're letting yourself in for before signing anything. **Remember** a job won't solve your money crisis if your money crisis is caused by spending money on things you don't really need. You'll just end up spending more. **Remember,** you *do* have to sleep, eat, travel, and write essays *sometime* ...

SEX 'N DRUGS 'N RAVE 'N ROLL

You're a clean-livin' Christian, always have been. *You* aren't going to jump into a student bedsit with the first hunk/chick you see. *You* aren't going to buy E's from the bouncer's mate at the Trocadero. *You* aren't going to supplement your income by offering personal services round the back of the railway station. *You* aren't going to be fondled by a lecturer up against the fume cupboard. *You* aren't going to drink fifteen bottles of Hooch and vomit all over the Senior Lecturer's Hush Puppies ....

That's all right then. I should skip this bit if I were you, in case it makes you blush. Ordinary mortals read this section ...
Ah, you're still here, then? Right, let's get down to it:

Sex - Look, it happens. At college, boy meets girl. Sometimes boy meets boy. Sometimes girl meets girl. They even have clubs, for goodness sake! You'll see posters encouraging you to 'explore your sexuality'. Some Student Unions issue free condoms with their fresher's material. Christians are not immune. Unless you're from another planet, chances are, sometime in your student life, you'll feel all gooey about someone else, and one thing leads to another. In fact, at college, one thing often leads to another. 'Cos you feel lonely, sometimes, right? And excited sometimes, right? And sometimes you sit on someone's bed late at night for a deep conversation and there's no one around, right?

> **On the other hand ... because everyone's talking about sex probably means there's more talk than sex.**

Here's a few tips:
1. Stick to your principles
2. Which means treating yourself and other people with respect
3. Which means being honest with yourself about your motives and desires
4. Which means remembering that love and sex are not the same thing
5. Which means telling someone if you're worried, pressurised or confused
6. Which means God's grace, first, middle, and last
7. Which means take good care of body, mind and spirit.
'nough said?

Drugs

Chances are someone will offer you some drugs when you get to College, if they haven't already. It's part of the scene. You probably know more about drugs than StudentWise. The only useful thing to be said is if you're worried about drugs, **don't struggle on your own** - *talk to someone quick.*

Alcohol

But alcohol's different, right? The college drink culture goes from 'all-you-can-drink-for-a-tenner' sessions in the Union bar, through Departmental end-of-term parties with cheese and wine, to cheap 'n cheerful bar lunches with a pint, to the occasional Christian society event with a discreet corner full of six-packs. You pays your money and you takes your choice. But ... you *do* pay your money; the latest fashion drink *is* a rip-off; most people *do* think Christians are boring enough without being teetotal as well. C'est la vie.

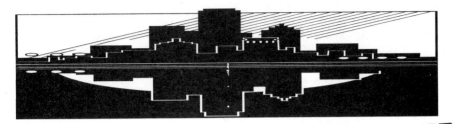

Crime

It goes on. Students are easy prey for criminals, both as victims and as potential recruits. Follow the advice of your Student Union, especially regarding travel and security. Report suspicious packages/people. Talk to someone before your money troubles get out of hand. Use your common sense when out late.

Sexual Harassment

This isn't the 1960's, when it was open season on sexual advances between staff and students (or so the stories say ...) But it still goes on. Your Student Union and Welfare department have policies on inappropriate behaviour. If you think you are on the wrong end of it, talk to someone you trust, follow the procedures.

Health

Even students at College suffer from ailments! Stress can cause illness. People get depressed. Shortage of funds leads some students to try managing on cheap not-very-nutritious food. The immune system weakens, result: colds, tiredness and tummy upsets! Then there's the serious stuff: drug and alcohol-related illnesses and sexually transmitted diseases are not unknown amongst students.

A general warning: look after yourself. Don't worry on your own. Don't neglect basic hygiene. Vary your diet and activities. Get enough sleep and exercise. Make sure you know where the health services are. Also, look out for your friends. If someone starts missing lectures, stays in their room, seems miserable and tired, or *just can't cope*, you may be able to persuade them to get help. You can certainly offer some support. *They may do the same thing for you one day ...*

CONCLUSION

This leaflet is only a guide, and it is offered in good faith to anyone who is leaving their home and friends to go to a college or university in a different part of the country. Time spent as a student should be, and in most cases is, an exciting, interesting and enjoyable time. For a Christian, the range of opportunities is every bit as great as for anyone else, though different in several respects, as will be clear by now. To sum up the advice of this pamphlet; take hold of your opportunities with open hands, and look for God's leading in and through them all. But if you get into difficulties, don't collapse under a weight of guilt (a special Christian tendency!), but ask for help, like anyone else would.

The college years are a good time for taking giant steps toward Christian maturity. Part of such maturity is learning to think for yourself, while learning that being Christian is about more than living for yourself. The Holy Spirit is at work as you study, learn, play, think, worship and serve. Maintain your relationship with Jesus through the Christian community and make new friends and explorations in the wider world, and you will have a fine student career, and be set on a good pathway for the life that lies before you. *Every good wish.*

CONTACTS

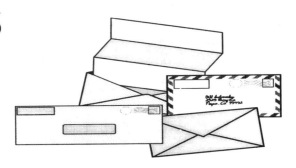

Chaplain _

Local minister _

Student welfare _

Health centre _

NOTES

Comments and suggestions for inclusion in future editions can be made to the Ministry Department, Baptist Union of Great Britain